MAK

MEALS

QUICK AND HEALTHY DINNER AND LUNCH RECIPES
LOW CARB, LOW CAL, LOW FAT

BY
JESSE MORGAN

Follow the link below
For a Free Food Safety Guide
Tips on shelf life
& cooking temperatures for common foods
AND
a free recipe from the book

http://fitrecipe.net/?p=75

TABLE OF CONTENTS

INTRODUCTION

Thank you for your interest in my latest book, Make Ahead Meals. Crazy day? Not ready to spend hours preparing a meal for your family? Are you struggling to figure out what to bring to lunch each day?

Purchase this book if you are looking for:

- Meals you can cook in advance and then heat up for lunch or dinner
- Healthy and Nutritious recipes that are easy to prepare
- Low carb, low calorie or low fat recipes

Each recipe includes the ingredients, complete instructions, prep and cook time, nutritional information and a flag to show if the meal is low carb or low fat.

My book Carb Cycling: The Recipe and Diet Book was well received on Amazon thanks in large part to the recipes that were included. My goal with this book is to provide recipes that can be used to support your current diet, help you find ways to eat healthier at lunch and dinner or just take some of the stress out of meal preparation.

If you have any questions or feedback, I would love to hear from you. If you find this book of value, please post a quick review on Amazon. A four or five star review will help drive sales which in turn will allow me to produce more great content for you and my other readers.

Please stop by my site www.FitRecipe.net and join our community for updates on my books and other topics around fitness, dieting and food. You will also find free content you can download including a dieting journal and a food safety guide.

One final note on reheating food in your microwave. Microwaves are not all the same, they have different power ranges. The suggestions in the book are based on my microwave, always check to make sure you food is heated throughout before eating.

*Jesse Morgan – **Jesse@FitRecipe.net***
www.fitrecipe.net

FRESHLY MADE VERSUS FROZEN MEALS WHICH IS BETTER?

The frozen entrée has become a staple in many people's diets. Ironically, in an era where time saving inventions seem to multiply at the speed of light, we seem to have less and less time to do those things that we want to do. Thus, being able to amble down the aisle of your local supermarket's frozen food section and toss in a week or two's worth of lunches and dinners is one way to save some of that precious time that you can then allot to something other than cooking.

However, the benefits attributed to the purchasing and consuming of frozen meals are slim, and the negatives overwhelmingly abundant. Frozen meals save time, there's an overall convenience factor, and many taste good. But the fact is with a little planning you can enjoy lunches made from fresh ingredients everyday and appreciate the enhanced benefits of doing so.

More Variety

In the frozen food section, what you see is what you get. You're confined to the choices offered by the various bulk manufactures of premade entrees. When you make your own lunches and dinners, you can create personalized dishes. The recipes in this book are a great starting point. They offer a fine range of choices, and there's no need to alter any of them.

However, if you do want to get creative, you can. With each recipe in this book, you may exchange and substitute ingredients, such as herbs and spices, vegetables, and types of oil, to create subtle differences in taste that fit perfectly with your palate. Also, the recipes may inspire you to create some of your own specialized dishes. The more experience you have in preparing food and cooking in a kitchen, the more proficient, knowledgeable, and confident you become, and the more likely you are to expand on your repertoire of recipes.

Healthier

One thing that choice gives you is control in preparing your own meals. When you cook, you certainly have the ability to manage what goes into each dish, and that means that you can make sound choices. Each recipe in this cookbook has been designed to be healthy. By making them you are learning firsthand what ingredients are better for you, and you are adopting them as part of a more beneficial lifestyle. If junk in results in junk out, as is the case with many frozen meals, imagine the results you'll feel and see from fueling your body with fresh ingredients that are good for you?

More Nutrients

Fresh ingredients, such as vegetables, poultry, fish, pork, and red meat, contain more nutrients than those that are frozen.

Frozen entrees tend to be deficient in offering adequate servings of fruits and vegetables, which contain so many of the vitamins and minerals that we need, and those fruits and vegetables that they do include often have the goodness cooked out of them. Additionally, you have control over the types of protein that you include in your meals, which means you can choose to include fresh caught fish, free range poultry, and non-steroid meats.

Better Fats

You can also control the type of fats you use. Frozen, precooked lunches and dinners often contain unhealthy fats. Many of the oils used in these foods are processed in ways that rob them of their essence. They may be put through a mechanical pressing process that is done at extremely high temperatures, or they may undergo bleaching, filtering and deodorizing. As fats are refined, they lose nutrients, and, at the same time, new, unwanted chemical compounds can result. Plus, the oils may have been extracted from plants that have been genetically modified and/or sprayed with pesticides. When you prepare meals on your own you are in charge of all ingredients, including fats.

No Junk Ingredients

Junk ingredients, those that have no healthful benefit or that are unhealthy, are prevalent in dishes sold in the frozen food section. Frozen meals will often have added flavorings, chemicals, preservatives, and gluten. Plus, many have large amounts of sodium, which is a major problem for those who have high blood pressure.

When you prepare your own meals you wont be adding extenders, fillers, or modifiers, plus, if it is important to you, you have the choice of buying fruits, vegetables and meats that have been organically grown and raised. The fact is by making your lunch or dinner you will automatically eliminate a large number of unnecessary and often unhealthy ingredients.

Eco-Friendly

If you want to help preserve the environment, you'll be doing so by reducing the use of the huge amounts of plastic and cardboard that is used in packaging frozen meals. The packaging is usually tossed away once the meals are consumed and crated off to landfills. You can store and transport your meals in reusable glass containers or, if you find them acceptable, reusable plastic containers.

Kitchen Fun and Creativity

If you're an inexperienced cook, the wonderful thing about the recipes in this cookbook is that they are not only quick to make and great tasting, but they are also easy even for a beginner. For many people cooking is an activity that they enjoy. There's a sense of accomplishment and satisfaction in creating meals. Thus, if the kitchen intimidates you, don't let it. Once you get started, you'll not only find the activity enjoyable, but, like many people, you'll discover that it's relaxing and perhaps even inspiring. Once you get a few hours under your belt, you may even start to improvise on the recipes in this book or create your own quick and healthy lunches and dinners.

If you are a seasoned cook, then you're already having fun, or at least you used to do so. You may be one of those people who stopped cooking due to the fact that they had to find time for other things. You can get back to the bliss you felt before with these fast recipes, while enjoying the benefits of a more healthy diet.

Less Expensive

Overall, fixing your own meals is less expensive. The recipes in this cookbook usually yield two or three servings. You can save even more money by making more servings and freezing them for future use. Usually beef, pork, and poultry is cheaper when purchased in larger quantities, plus you'll use less energy if you make more servings at once. Although, as mentioned earlier in this chapter, freezing will lower the nutritional value to a degree, the fact that you've made these meals yourself from fresh ingredients will still put you ahead in the mineral and vitamin count.

Saving Time

We also noted at the beginning of this chapter that one of the positive factors in purchasing meals in your supermarket's frozen food department is that it saves time. There's nothing easier than opening one of the glass freezer doors in your store's frozen food aisle and reaching for those entrées you know so well. But there are also ways to save time even with these already quick to make recipes.

Take a moment to plan what you are going to prepare for the week. Organize the information and the recipes. Also, carefully arrange the preparation. As an example, if you're going to make the One Pan Chicken Fajitas recipe, you may also want to cook up Turkey Chili, since the chili can be cooking while you're preparing the other entrée. An additional way to save time would be to add a third recipe to your cooking session that utilizes one of the same sources of protein. In this case, it would be either chicken or turkey.

You can save more time by doubling the recipes and freezing servings of all three. That would give you six servings of each, which you could have over the course of a month of so. A little bit of planning will go a long way to conserve time, which is so precious.

Enjoy Your Homemade Meals

With a little bit of effort, you can have a freshly made lunch or dinner anytime you want. It will taste better and be healthier than eating meals selected from the frozen food department of your market. Enjoy the results of what will be fun and light labor. In our fast-paced, throw away world, these quick recipes are exceptionally fulfilling.

PRESERVING YOUR FRESHLY MADE MEALS PROPER STORAGE IS IMPORTANT

If you are preparing one of the quick recipes in this cookbook for tomorrow's lunch or dinner or are cooking numerous servings to freeze and enjoy over a period of time, it's important to store your meals in the proper manner. This will preserve freshness and stop the spread of harmful bacteria, which can cause food poisoning. In this chapter, we'll consider some basic food preparation safety tips, as well as how to best preserve your meals once they are cooked.

Food Prep Safety

When preparing food, always follow proper food prep hygiene, including carefully washing cutting boards and knives between uses. If you've just been handling any type of meat, poultry, or fish, wash your hands with warm, soapy water and dry them before handling fresh vegetables, fruits, or other foods. Also, never leave meat, poultry, fish, milk or other such products out of the refrigerator for an extended period of time.

Wash any fresh fruits or vegetables before cutting them, as this will help prevent food poisoning. As an example, if you cut a cantaloupe without first washing the skin harmful salmonella bacteria on the outside of the melon can be carried into the fruit by the knife blade, contaminating it. Use common sense when prepping a meal and always be wary of cross-contamination hazards.

Refrigerator Storage

Store cooked foods in your refrigerator. Your refrigerator should be set at 40-degrees Fahrenheit. It's a good idea to keep a refrigerator thermometer in your unit to monitor the temperature. In many refrigerators, the lower shelves and drawers will be cooler than those in the middle or upper areas. This is why you'll find vegetable crispers at floor level and meat storage units closer to the middle of the unit.

Store cooked foods in airtight containers and, if you are taking your meals to work or out of the home, place individual servings in their own storage receptacles. Although plastic storage bags or plastic wrap work well for sandwiches, most entrées will hold their shape best if stored in reusable glass or plastic containers. The better the seal, the fresher your meal will be and the longer it will be preserved.

Meals that contain cooked beef, poultry, chicken or pork, and cream dishes will last three to four days when refrigerated. Other dishes, such as rice, noodles, and cooked vegetables, will stay fresh a little longer. However, it is always safest to consume cooked food within four days of preparation.

Fresh, uncut vegetables and fruits can usually be stored for a week. Although you can make fresh salads ahead of time and store them in the fridge, uncooked vegetables and fruits retain their freshness longer and taste better if they remain whole until just being served. If you make a salad ahead of time, it will stay fresh from two to four days and not for a week.

Freezing Meals

Preparing freezer-ready meals will save you time and offer convenience in terms of your being able to enjoy a quick lunch or dinner any time that you want one. Store individual servings in their own containers and then you can simply take one for lunch and pop it in the microwave when you're ready to eat. You can also remove foods from the freezer and place them in the fridge to defrost overnight.

Here are some food storage tips for your freezer:

- For convenience use containers that are both freezer and microwave safe.
- Food should cool completely before being put into containers. Placing cooked foods in containers and freezing them when the outside is cool but the center is still warm can promote bacteria growth.
- With soups, chili dishes, and sauces, leave some room in the container for expansion during freezing.
- Vegetables should be undercooked a bit if freezing, as this will prevent them from being too soft and mushy when they are reheated in the microwave.

- Make your packaging as airtight as possible. This will help prevent freezer burn, which, although not unhealthy, will compromise the look and texture of your food.
- Label each dish and date it.
- Rotate food in your freezer, putting the items that have most recently been prepared in the back and those that are older towards the front.
- To track effectively, keep an inventory of and track the consumption of your frozen meals. This will help reduce waste.
- Read your freezer manual to see what your unit's optimum fill level is, as some perform best when completely full, while others are more efficient when being partially used.
- To maximize taste and freshness, consume dishes within one month.
- As a general rule of thumb:
    o Fruits and vegetables will last up to eight months in a freezer.
    o Fish and shellfish for up to six months.
    o Meat and poultry for three months.
- Never risk food poisoning by consuming food that has been frozen for too long or that has had its packaging compromised.
- Never refreeze meals you have defrosted, as this will result in the degrading of the texture and taste, and it can promote the growth of bacteria.

There are many cooked items that can be frozen successfully. These include:

- Baked goods
- Beans
- Various types of burgers
- Burritos
- Calzones
- Casseroles
- Chili
- Grains
- Egg rolls
- Enchiladas
- Fajitas
- Lasagna
- Manicotti
- Mashed potatoes
- Meatballs
- Meatloaf
- Pot pies,
- Poultry dishes
- Quiche
- Ravioli
- Roasted meats
- Sauces
- Soups
- Stuffed shells
- Taco fillings

Foods that tend to not freeze well include:

- Cream-based sauces
- Egg-based sauces
- Instant rice
- Fried foods
- Hard-cooked eggs
- Stuffed poultry or pork
- Uncooked, water-filled vegetables such as celery, lettuce, and tomatoes

If you are unsure if a meal will do well in the freezer, a good idea is to test freeze a small portion of it to see how it does. That way if the taste and texture don't hold up you haven't lost the entire meal.

Careful Prep and Storage

By taking some care and using common sense in preparing and storing your quick and healthy meals, you'll be able to enjoy fresh made lunches and dinners anytime. Follow the guidelines in this chapter and always practice sound food safety practices.

RECIPES

Chicken In The Oven

LOW FAT

4 Servings | Prep-time: 10 minutes | Cook-time: 45 minutes

Ingredients:

1 large Vidalia onion

2 cups baby carrots

2 large potatoes

2 green peppers

4 boneless, skinless, chicken breasts

1/2 cup white wine

3 cloves garlic

1 teaspoon each, salt and pepper

1 tablespoon Italian seasonings

Instructions:

1) Preheat oven to 400 degrees. Line a large baking dish with tinfoil. Peel onion, slice in half, and then slice each half into six equal wedges. Add onion and baby carrots to the bottom of the baking dish. Wash peppers, remove seeds and stems and cut into small cubes, about the size of the onion. Add to the baking dish.

2) Rinse the chicken breasts and lay them on top of the vegetables, space them out across the pan so that none of the chicken breasts are overlapping.

3) Pour wine over the chicken and vegetables, mince garlic cloves with a garlic press of by chopping finely with your knife and sprinkle over the chicken. Sprinkle over the salt, pepper, and Italian seasonings.

Cover baking dish with tinfoil and transfer to the oven.

4) Bake chicken covered for 30 minutes, remove foil and bake for an additional 10-20 minutes, until chicken is no longer pink on the inside.

5) Enjoy chicken right away or portion equally into four separate microwave safe portable containers. To reheat simply microwave for 1-2 minutes, until chicken and vegetables are hot.

Nutrition Facts (Per serving)

Calories: 362
Fat: 3g
Carbs: 45g
Protein: 35g
Sodium: 662mg
Sugar: 9g

Baked Lemon Chicken with Broccoli

LOW FAT/LOW CARB
2 Servings | Prep-time: 10 minutes | Cook-time: 30 minutes

Ingredients:

1 pound chicken tenderloins
2 lemons
3 cloves garlic, minced
1 teaspoon Dijon mustard
1/2 teaspoon black pepper
1/4 teaspoon salt
3 cups broccoli florets

Instructions:

1) Preheat oven to 400 degrees. Rinse chicken tenderloins, pat dry with a paper towel, and slice each tenderloin into four small pieces. Place chicken into a nonstick baking dish.

2) Using a zester or grater, zest one of the lemons and add the zest to the chicken. Slice both of the lemons in half and juice, using a fork, over the chicken. Add garlic, mustard, pepper, and salt to the chicken. Using your hands, rub the chicken to make sure each piece is evenly coated. Transfer baking dish to the oven and set the timer for 25 minutes. While chicken is cooking, place broccoli into a glass microwaves safe bowl, add 1/2 cup of water and cover with plastic wrap. Microwave the broccoli for 1 1/2 minutes on high or if you prefer you can steam the broccoli.

3) Once the chicken has baked for 25 minutes, remove from the oven and stir in the broccoli. Transfer the chicken and broccoli back to the oven and cook for an additional five minutes.

4) Divide the chicken and broccoli into three portions, you can enjoy right away or place each portion into a microwave safe plastic or glass portable container. To reheat, simply place in the microwave for 1 minute, stir, microwave for an additional minute, and enjoy.

Nutrition Fats (Per serving)

Calories: 275
Fat: 2.5g
Carbs: 12.5g
Protein: 56g
Sodium 520mg
Sugar: 3.5g

Baked Pesto Chicken

LOW FAT/LOW CARB
2 Servings | Prep-time: 5 minutes | Cook-time: 25 minutes

Ingredients:

2 boneless, skinless, chicken breasts
2 tablespoons store bought pesto
1 Roma tomato

Instructions:

1) Heat oven to 400 degrees. Rinse chicken breasts and pat dry with a paper towel. Spray a nonstick baking sheet with cooking spray and lay chicken breasts down on it.

2) Using a cooking brush or butter knife, spread 1 tablespoon of pesto over the top of each chicken breast. Rinse the Roma tomato and slice into six thin

slices. Lay three slices over each breast and transfer the chicken to the oven.

3) Bake chicken for 25 minutes, enjoy with a side salad or steamed 2 cups vegetables of your choice. You can enjoy the chicken right away or place each breast into a microwave safe, portable container, and reheat in the microwave when ready to eat for 1 to 11/2 minutes.

Nutrition Facts (Per serving)

Calories: 240
Fat: 10g
Carbs: 5g
Protein: 32g
Sodium: 207mg
Sugar: 3g

One Pan Chicken Fajitas

LOW FAT
3 Servings | Prep-time: 15 minutes | Cook-time: 15 minutes

Ingredients:

1 pound chicken tenderloins

1 large green pepper

1 large red or yellow pepper

1 large Vidalia onion

2 cloves garlic

2 tablespoons fajita seasonings

1 tablespoon olive oil

2 small corn tortilla shells per serving

Optional toppings:

Sliced avocado

Reduced-fat cheddar or monetary jack cheese

Fat-free refried beans

Fresh chopped tomatoes

Fresh cilantro

Diced red onion

Fat-free plain Greek yogurt

Salsa

Instructions:

1) Rinse chicken and pat dry with a paper towel. Slice tenders into thirds and set aside.

2) On a separate, clean, cutting board, take the tops off of the peppers, slice them in half and scoop the seeds out. Slice peppers into thin slices, about 1/4-1/2 inch thick. Take the peel off of the onion, slice it in half so that it lays flat on the cutting board, and slice each half into thin slices, about the same thickness as the peppers. Next, either mince garlic using a garlic press or simply chop finely with your knife.

   *Now that you have all of your ingredients chopped, you can cook the meal right away or you can freeze it for later (directions below)

3) Place a large pan over medium heat and add the olive oil. Once hot, add your chicken tenderloins, peppers, onion, garlic, and fajita seasonings. Cook, stirring often, until the chicken is no longer pink and the peppers and onions have softened, about 15 minutes.

4) Microwave the tortilla shells for 15 seconds to warm and soften them. Scoop your chicken fajita mixture into the tortilla shells and top with optional toppings of your choice, enjoy!

   *You can easily heat up the leftovers by simply putting them in the microwave for 1 minute and then putting inside the warmed tortilla shells. This makes this meal perfect to bring for lunch or for a quick, make ahead, dinner after a busy day.

Instructions for freezing: This meal can easily be prepared ahead and frozen for when you are ready to cook it. Perform steps 1 and 2 just as listed above. Instead of moving on to step 3, add chicken, peppers, onions, garlic, and seasonings to a large freezer bag and pop it in the freezer! When you are ready to make this, transfer your ingredients from the freezer to the fridge in the morning and they will be perfectly defrosted come dinner time! This allows you to skip ahead to step 3 when you are ready to cook and avoid the prep-work and extra clean up.

Nutrition Facts (per serving)

Calories: 346
Fat: 7g
Carbs: 32g
Protein: 39g
Sodium: 600mg
Sugar: 6g

Cashew Chicken

LOW FAT
2 Servings | Prep-time: 15 minutes | Cook-time: 25-30

Ingredients:

2 boneless, skinless, chicken breasts
1/2 medium Vidalia onion
2 cloves garlic
1 teaspoon sesame oil
1 cup chicken stock
2 cups broccoli florets
2 tablespoons light brown sugar
2 tablespoons soy sauce
1 teaspoon ground ginger
1/2 teaspoon crushed red pepper
2 tablespoons chopped cashews
1 cup pre-cooked brown rice

Instructions:

1) Rinse chicken and pat dry with a paper towel. Slice into thin strips. Chop onion finely. Mince garlic either using a garlic press or by chopping finely.

2) Heat a nonstick pan over medium heat and add chicken, onion, garlic, and sesame oil. Cook, stirring constantly, until chicken is no longer pink.

3) Add chicken stock, broccoli, brown sugar, soy sauce, ginger, and red pepper to the pan, reduce heat to medium-low and cover. Cook until broccoli is tender, stirring occasionally, for about 15 minutes, once cooked, stir in chopped cashews and remove from heat.

4) Serve over 1/2 cup brown rice. Enjoy right away or distribute evenly into two separate microwave safe, portable containers. To reheat simply microwave for 1 1/2 minutes and enjoy.

Nutrition Facts (Per serving):

Calories: 442
Fat: 9g
Carbs: 51g
Protein: 38g
Sodium: 1385mg
Sugar: 18g

Crock Pot Chicken Marsala

LOW FAT/LOW CARB
4 Servings | Prep-time: 15 minutes | Cook-time: 6-8 hour

Ingredients:

4 skinless, boneless, chicken breasts

1 medium Vidalia onion

2 cloves garlic

4 cups sliced button mushrooms

2 tablespoons cornstarch

1 cup chicken stock

1/2 cup Marsala win

1 teaspoon ground thyme

1 tablespoon fresh or dried parsley

1/2 teaspoon rosemary

1 teaspoon garlic powder

1/2 teaspoon each, salt and pepper

Instructions:

1) Rinse chicken breasts and pat dry with a paper towel. Slice chicken breasts in half across, so that they are thinner but the same width. Lay chicken breasts down into your crockpot.

2) Peel the onion, slice in half and then into thin slices. Mince the garlic either with a garlic press or by chopping finely. Lay onions, garlic, and mushrooms on top of the chicken. Mix the cornstarch into the chicken broth until it dissolves and pour over the chicken, along with the wine.

3) Cook for 6-8 hours on low, you can prep this in the morning and it will be ready to eat when you get home!

4) To enjoy later, simply portion chicken Marsala into microwave safe, portable containers and reheat in the microwave for 1 1/2 - 2 minutes, until hot, enjoy.

Nutrition Facts (Per serving):

Calories: 222
Fat: 3g
Carbs: 11g
Protein: 35g
Sodium: 358mg
Sugar: 4g

Grilled Chicken Salad

LOW FAT/LOW CARB
2 Servings | Prep-time: 10 minutes | Cook-time:16 minutes

Ingredients:

2 skinless, boneless, chicken breasts

1 large stalk celery

1/4 teaspoon each, salt and pepper

2 tablespoons olive oil mayonnaise

2 teaspoons dried dill

3 low-carb pita pockets

2-3 leaves romaine lettuce for each pocket

Instructions:

1) Preheat grill to medium heat and spray with nonstick spray. Rinse chicken breasts and pat dry with a paper towel. Grill each breast for about 8 minutes on each side, or until it has an internal temperature of 165 degrees.

2) While the chicken is cooking, rinse the celery and chop into very small dices.

3) Once chicken is fully cooked, remove from grill and allow to cool. Cut chicken into small bite-sized pieces. Transfer to a mixing bowl.

4) Add diced celery, salt, pepper, mayonnaise, and dill and mix using a spoon until each piece of chicken is well coated.

5) Slice pita pockets at the top, lay a few slices of lettuce inside of each, and scoop an even amount of chicken salad into each pocket. To bring for lunch, simply wrap your pocket in tinfoil or plastic wrap, refrigerate until you are ready to eat, and enjoy!

Nutrition Facts (Per serving)

Calories: 210
Fat: 7g
Carbs: 12g
Protein: 27g
Sodium: 423mg
Sugar: 2g

Massaged Kale Salad with Grilled Chicken

2 Servings |Prep-time: 10 minutes |Cook-time: n/a

Ingredients:

2 lemons
1/2 avocado
1/4 tsp salt
1/2 tsp pepper
1 bunch kale leaves, stems removed
1/2 cup red grapes, halved
1/4 cup walnuts, chopped
2 boneless, skinless, grilled chicken breasts*

Instructions:

1) Using a zester or grater, zest 1/2 of 1 lemon into a mixing bowl. Slice the lemons in half and juice them, using a fork, into the bowl. Add the avocado, salt, and pepper.

2) Using a fork, mash the avocado and mix until all lumps are gone and it forms a thick, dressing-like consistency.

3) Next, wash the kale and cut it into thin slices. Add the kale to your dressing bowl and massage the dressing into the kale with your hands. Make sure the dressing is thoroughly distributed, as the juice of the lemon will help to tenderize the kale.

4) Next, add grapes, walnuts, and chicken and toss. You can eat right away, or store the salad in containers for an on-the-go lunch or dinner. Enjoy!

*You can find pre-cooked chicken breasts at the grocery store if you do not have time to grill them yourself!

To grill the chicken breasts yourself. Preheat your grill to medium heat. Rinse the chicken with water and pat dry with a paper towel. Lay chicken breasts on a plate and sprinkle each with salt, pepper, and garlic powder. Transfer chicken to grill and grill for about 8-10 minutes on each side, until they reach a temperature of 170 to 180 degrees. You can use the grilled chicken right away or freeze the cooked chicken, which can easily be defrosted in the microwave or by sitting overnight in the fridge.

Nutrition Facts (per serving)

Calories: 368
Fat: 14g
Carbs: 30g
Protein: 38g
Sodium: 105mg
Sugar: 8g

Chicken Salad with Apples and Walnuts

2 Servings |Prep-time: 10 minutes |Cook-time: n/a

Ingredients:

1 boneless, skinless chicken breast, grilled*
8 cups green leafy lettuce
2 ribs celery
1/2 large green apple
1 ounce chopped walnuts
2 tablespoons raisins
1/4 cup low-fat Italian dressing

Instructions

1) Wash and dry lettuce and place onto two separate plates, or into two portable containers. Chop chicken breast into small cubes and distribute evenly between the two salads.

2) Slice celery into thin pieces, chop apple into bit-sized pieces and add half the celery, half the apple, and half the walnuts onto each salad. Top with 1 tablespoons raisins each.

3) Drizzle over 2 tablespoons Italian dressing when you are ready to serve, if you are taking for lunch make sure to keep dressing on the side until ready to eat to keep the salad from becoming soggy.

*You can buy pre-cooked grilled chicken breasts at most grocery stores, or follow the directions from recipe #1 to grill the chicken breasts yourself.

Nutrition Facts (Per serving):

Calories: 293
Fat: 13g
Carbs: 26g
Protein: 20g
Sodium: 413mg
Sugar: 18

Meatball Parmesan

3 Servings | Prep-time: 10 minutes | Cook-time: 20 minutes

Ingredients:

1 pound 90/10 ground hamburger meat

1 large egg

1/4 cup Italian breadcrumbs

2 tablespoons ketchup

1 tablespoon Worcestershire sauce

1 tablespoon dried Italian seasonings

1 tablespoon dried onion

1 teaspoon garlic powder

3 ounces fresh mozzarella cheese

1 cup marinara sauce

Instructions:

1) Preheat oven to 350 degrees.

2) In a large mixing bowl, add meat, egg, breadcrumbs, ketchup, Worcestershire sauce, and seasonings. Using your hands, mix until all ingredients are well combined.

3) Form into 12 round meatballs and place on a nonstick baking sheet. Bake for 15 minutes, flip and bake for an additional 5 minutes.

4) While meatballs are cooking, slice mozzarella into 12 equal slices. Remove meatballs from oven, top each with sauce and a slice of cheese. Bake for an additional 5 minutes to melt cheese.

5) Once cooled, store meatballs, in portions of four, in microwave safe portable containers.

6) To reheat, simply place meatballs, in their container, in the microwave for 1 minutes, and enjoy!

Nutrition Fats (Per serving)

Calories: 506
Fat: 35g
Carbs: 22g
Protein: 38g
Sodium: 1136mg
Sugar: 7g

Southwest Meatballs over Zucchini Noodles

LOW FAT
4 Servings | Prep-time: 20 minutes | Cook-time: 15 minutes

Ingredients:

1/2 small onion
1/4 cup cilantro
1/2 cup canned black beans
1/2 cup canned or frozen corn
1 pound lean ground turkey
1/4 cup low-fat cheddar cheese
1/2 teaspoon each, salt and pepper
1 teaspoon garlic powder
1/2 teaspoon cumin
4 large zucchinis

Instructions:

1) Preheat oven to 400 degrees. Chop onion into very small pieces. Chop cilantro. Rinse black beans and corn with water to remove excess sodium. Transfer

onion, cilantro, black beans, and corn into a large mixing bowl. Add the ground turkey, cheddar cheese, salt, pepper, garlic powder, and cumin.

2) Mix the turkey mixture together, using your hands, until everything is well combined. Form into 16 small meatballs and place on a nonstick baking dish.

3) Transfer to oven and bake for 15 minutes.

4) While the meatballs are cook, use a spiralizer to spiralize the zucchini. Place zucchini in a large bowl, add 1/2 cup water, and cover with plastic wrap. Microwave noodles for two minutes, so that they are soft but not overcooked.

5) Once meatballs are ready, enjoy over the zucchini noodles right away, or separate evenly between four microwave safe portable containers. To reheat, simply microwave for 1 1/2 minutes, until the noodles and meatballs are hot, enjoy!

Nutrition Facts (Per serving):

Calories: 262
Fat: 10g
Carbs: 20g
Protein: 28g
Sodium: 479mg
Sugar: 9g

Crock Pot Beef Stew

LOW FAT
4 Servings |Prep-time: 15 minutes |Cook-time: 6-8 hours

Ingredients

1 pound beef stew meat
2 large red potatoes
4 large carrots
4 large celery ribs
1 Vidalia onion
1/2 cup frozen peas
1 tablespoon Worcestershire sauce
1/2 teaspoon each, salt and pepper
1 tablespoon dried parsley
1 teaspoon oregano
2 teaspoons garlic powder

Instructions:

1) Rinse beef stew meat and potatoes and cut into small, bite-sized pieces. Peel the carrots, rinse the celery,

and slice across into 1/2 inch thick pieces. Peel the onion, slice in half, and then chop roughly. Add all of these ingredients into the crockpot along with the frozen peas.

2) Add the Worcestershire sauce and seasoning into the crockpot and pour over 1 cup of water. Mix a few times to make sure everything is well combined and cover.

3) Cook on high heat for 6-8 hours. If you turn the crockpot on in the morning your beef stew will be waiting for you to enjoy for dinner!

4) Once cooked, enjoy beef stew right away or divide into four separate, microwave safe, portable containers. To reheat, simply place container in the microwave, cook for one minute, stir, cook for an additional minute and enjoy.

Nutrition Facts (Per serving)

Calories: 337
Fat: 6g
Carbs: 37.5g
Protein: 29g
Sodium: 492mg
Sugar: 5g

Sausage & Zucchini Stew

LOW FAT
4 Servings | Prep-time: 10 minutes | Cook-time: 1 hours, 10 minutes

Ingredients:

3 links fresh turkey sausage

1 medium Vidalia onion

1/2 cup water

2 cloves garlic

2 large zucchinis

3 celery ribs

2 large russet potatoes

1 can low-sodium white beans

1, 14.5 ounce, can diced tomatoes

1 teaspoon garlic powder

1 teaspoon oregano

1 teaspoon black pepper

1/4 teaspoon cayenne pepper

Instructions:

1) Slice sausage links into bite sized pieces. Peel onion and chop roughly. Add onion and sausage into a large sauce pan over medium heat. Cook until lightly browned, about 5 minutes, and then add 1/2 cup water. Continue cooking for another 5 minutes.

2) Mince garlic either with a garlic press or by chopping finely, and add to the pot. Slice zucchini, celery, and potatoes, into small, bite-sized pieces. Add to the pan, along with all remaining ingredients.

3) Reduce heat to medium-low, cover, and cook for 1 hour, stirring occasionally. Enjoy right away or portion equally into four microwave safe, portable containers. To reheat, simply microwave for 1 1/2 minutes, stir, microwave for an additional minute and enjoy.

Nutrition Facts (Per serving):

Calories: 370
Fat: 5g
Carbs: 65g
Protein: 20g
Sodium: 1,000mg
Sugar: 12g

Cheesesteak Stuffed Peppers

LOW CARB
2 Servings | Prep-time: 8 minutes | Cook-time: 28 minutes

Ingredients:

2 cloves garlic

1 medium Vidalia onion

12 ounces fresh shaved steak

1 tablespoon Worcestershire sauce

1/2 teaspoon black pepper

2 large green peppers

4 thin slices provolone cheese

Instructions:

1) Preheat oven to 375 degrees. Mince garlic either with a garlic press or by chopping finely with a knife. Peel onion, slice in half and then slice each half into thin slices.

2) Place a nonstick pan over medium heat and add

steak, garlic, and onions. Cook for five minutes and then stir in the Worcestershire sauce and pepper, cook for an additional 2-3 minutes, it is okay if the steak is still a little pink.

3) Slice the green peppers in half, lengthwise, and scoop out the seeds. Lay peppers down onto a baking dish and fill each pepper evenly with 1/4 of the steak. Top peppers with a slice of provolone cheese.

4) Bake for 20 minutes, until the peppers have softened. You can enjoy them right away or place two pepper halves each into microwavable, portable containers. To reheat simply microwave for 1 1/2 to 2 minutes, until the centers are warm.

Nutrition Facts (Per serving)

Calories: 370
Fat: 18g
Carbs: 13g
Protein: 41g
Sodium: 437mg
Sugar: 6g

Pepper Steak

LOW CARB

3 Servings |Prep-time: 15 minutes |Cook-time: 15-20 minutes

Ingredients:

1 large red pepper
1 large green pepper
1 large Vidalia onion
1 tablespoon vegetable oil
12 ounces flank steak
2 cloves garlic, minced
2 tablespoons cornstarch
1 tablespoon soy sauce
1/2 teaspoon ground ginger
1/2 teaspoon black pepper

Instructions:

1) Cut the stems off of the peppers and scoop the seeds out. Peel the onion, slice the peppers and onion into long thin strips.

2) Heat a large nonstick pan over medium-high heat and add the oil. Once the oil is hot, add the peppers and onion and cook for five minutes, stirring often.

3) While the peppers and onions are cooking, slice the steak into long thin pieces, similar to the size of the peppers. Once the peppers and onions have cooked for five minutes, add the steak.

4) Cook just until the steak is no longer pink. Stir the cornstarch with the soy sauce to dissolve and add to steak, along with ground ginger and pepper. Stir and

then remove from heat.

5) Enjoy steak right away or portion into three separate microwave safe, portable plastic or glass containers.

*If you like, enjoy the pepper steak with a small baked potato, 1/2 cup cooked brown rice, or two small corn tortilla shells.

Nutrition facts (Per serving)

Calories: 364
Fat: 21g
Carbs: 14.5g
Protein: 30g
Sodium: 553mg
Sugar: 4g

Flatbread pizza

1 Servings |Prep-time: 6-8 minutes |Cook-time: 12 minutes

Ingredients:

1 Syrian flatbread

1/2 cup pasta sauce

1/2 cup shredded low-fat mozzarella cheese

5 slices turkey pepperoni

Vegetables of choice for topping (peppers, onion, mushrooms, tomato, arugula, spinach, etc.)

Instructions:

1) Preheat oven to 375 degrees.

2) Lay Syrian bread down onto a nonstick baking sheet. Spread sauce onto the Syrian bread and sprinkle the cheese over the top. Lay on the turkey pepperoni and any vegetables of choice. Transfer to the oven.

3) Bake the pizza for 12 minutes. It is best enjoy right away, however these pizzas can be easily reheated in a toaster oven or by microwaving for 30 seconds.

Nutrition Facts:

Calories: 349

Fat: 19g

Carbs: 45g

Protein: 24g

Sodium: 1608mg

Sugar: 6g

Turkey Club Pinwheels

1 Servings |Prep-time: 5 minutes |Cook-time: n/a

Ingredients:

1 Roma tomato
1 low-carb wrap
1 tablespoon olive oil mayonnaise
1 cup chopped romaine lettuce
3 slices microwave bacon
4 ounce sliced deli turkey

Instructions:

1) Rinse tomato and slice into thin pieces. Lay down wrap and spread mayonnaise across it. Lay the tomatoes across the wrap and top with shredded lettuce.

2) Microwave the bacon for 30 seconds and place onto wrap. Lay turkey evenly over the wrap, fold in the ends, and then roll up.

3) Slice wrap into four "pinwheels" and refrigerate until you are ready to eat, enjoy.

Nutrition Facts:

Calories: 349
Fat: 18g
Carbs: 17g
Protein: 38g
Sodium: 1356mg
Sugar: 9g

Turkey Chili

LOW FAT
3 Servings |Prep-time: 10 minutes |Cook-time: 30 minutes

Ingredients:

1 tablespoon olive oil
1/2 cup white onion, chopped
1 pound lean ground turkey
1 green pepper, chopped
1 14.5ounce can red beans
1 14.5 ounce can diced tomatoes
1 package chili seasonings

Instructions:

1) Heat a nonstick pan over medium heat and add oil. Once hot, add onion and cook for 1 minute.

2) Add ground turkey and peppers and cook, using a wooden spoon to break up turkey.

3) Continue cooking the turkey until it is no longer pink, about ten minutes. Once cooked, stir in the red beans, tomatoes, and chili seasonings.

4) Lower heat to medium-low and continue cooking chili for another 15 minutes, stirring often.

5) Remove chili from heat and allow to cool for 15 minutes. Spoon turkey evenly into three separate microwave safe portable containers.

6) To reheat chili, microwave for 1 minute, stir, and microwave for an additional 45 seconds, enjoy!

Nutrition Fats (Per serving)

Calories: 394
Fat: 7g
Carbs: 37g
Protein: 45g
Sodium: 1,000mg
Sugar: 7g

Baked Stuffed Shrimp

LOW FAT
3 Servings |Prep-time: 12 minutes |Cook-time: 12 minutes

Ingredients

1 pound large or jumbo raw shrimp, peeled and deveined
1 lemon
2 ribs celery
1/2 small onion
3 cloves garlic
2 tablespoons butte
1 teaspoon Italian seasonings
1/4 cup white wine
1/4 cup chicken stock
1 cup panko breadcrumbs
1/2 teaspoon each, salt and pepper

Instructions:

1) Preheat the oven to 400 degrees. Spray a nonstick baking dish with cooking spray. Rinse shrimp and

remove tails, then lay them onto the baking dish. Slice lemon in half and juice oven the shrimp.

2) Slice celery and onion into small dices. Mince garlic either using a garlic press or by chopping finely with a knife. Melt butter over medium heat in a nonstick pan and add the celery onion and garlic. Cook for five minutes, stirring often.

3) Once vegetables have softened, add Italian seasonings, wine, and chicken stock. Cook for a minute and then turn off the heat and stir in the panko, salt, and pepper.

4) Spoon the stuffing mixture over the shrimp so that each shrimp has stuffing on top of it. Transfer dish to oven and bake for about 12 minutes. Enjoy with a side of steamed vegetables or salad.

5) You can enjoy the shrimp right away or portion into three separate microwave safe portable containers. To reheat simply microwave for 1 minute and enjoy.

Nutrition Facts (Per serving)

Calories: 297
Fat: 10g
Carbs: 20g
Protein: 37g
Sodium: 299mg
Sugar: 2g

Cilantro Lime Grilled Shrimp

LOW FAT/LOW CARB
3 Servings | Prep-time: 10 minutes | Cook-time: 8 minutes

Ingredients:

1 lime
1/2 cup fresh cilantro
1/4 teaspoon each, salt and pepper
1/2 teaspoon red pepper flake
1 pound large or jumbo shrimp, peeled and deveined
1 pound asparagus
2 teaspoons olive oil
1 teaspoon garlic powder

Instructions:

1) Preheat grill to medium. Zest half of the lime and transfer zest to a large bowl. Slice lime in half and juice into the bowl. Finely chop the cilantro, add to bowl along with the salt, pepper, and red pepper

flakes. Stir to combine, add the shrimp and stir to make sure each shrimp is coated.

2) Cut the ends off of the asparagus and rub with olive oil and garlic pepper. Place the shrimp on skewers and then transfer the skewers and the asparagus to the grill.

3) Grill for 4 minutes, flip the shrimp and asparagus, and grill for another 4 minutes.

4) Enjoy right away or split shrimp into three separate microwave safe portable containers. To reheat, simply microwave for 1- 1 1/2 minutes and enjoy!

Nutrition Facts (Per serving):

Calories: 177
Fat: 6g
Carbs: 6g
Protein: 38g
Sodium: 500mg
Sugar: 3g

Roasted Vegetable and Hummus Wrap

2 Servings |Prep-time: 12 minutes |Cook-time: 30 minutes

Ingredients:

1 large zucchini

1 large summer squash

1 small red onion

1 red pepper

1/2 pound asparagus

1 tablespoon olive oil

1/2 teaspoon each, salt and pepper

1 teaspoon garlic powder

1 teaspoon Italian seasonings

1/2 cup hummus

2 low-carb wraps or Syrian bread

Instructions:

1) Preheat oven to 400 degrees. Slice zucchini, squash, red onion, and red pepper into long, thin strips. Trip the ends off of the asparagus. Place the vegetables on a nonstick baking pan and rub with oil, salt, pepper, garlic powder, and Italian seasonings. Transfer to oven.

2) Bake vegetables for 25 minutes and then allow to cool for a few minutes.

3) Heat your tortilla or wrap in the microwave for 10 seconds to soften. Spread 1/4 cup of hummus on each wrap and fill them with the roasted vegetables. Roll the wraps up, and enjoy! You can also prepare

these wraps in advance and simply microwave for 30 seconds to warm up before eating.

Nutrition Facts (Per serving):

Calories: 352
Fat: 18g
Carbs: 40g
Protein: 11g
Sodium: 383mg
Sugar: 10g

Low-Carb Mac and Cheese

LOW FAT
4 Servings | Prep-time: 15 minutes | Cook-time: 20 minutes

Ingredients:

1 1/2 large heads of cauliflower (about 7 cups total)
1, 12 ounce box, frozen pureed butternut squash
1 cup chicken stock
1 cup fat-free milk
1 cup shredded low-fat sharp cheddar cheese
1/2 cup shredded parmesan cheese
1 teaspoon ground thyme
2 teaspoons garlic powder
1/2 teaspoon each, salt and pepper
1 teaspoon paprika
2 tablespoons dried onion

Instructions:

1) Heat a large pot of water over high heat. Meanwhile, slice the cauliflower into very small pieces, about the

size of elbow pasta in a typical mac and cheese. Once the water is boiling, drop the cauliflower in and cook for five minutes. Drain and set aside.

2) Heat oven to 375 degrees. Place a saucepan over medium heat and add the pureed butternut squash, chicken stock, milk, cheese, and seasonings. Cook over medium heat, stirring constantly, until the cheese has melted and a thick sauce has form, about 8-10 minutes.

3) Once your sauce is done, stir in the cauliflower until each piece is well coated. Transfer to a large nonstick baking dish and bake for 20 minutes.

4) Enjoy right away or portion the mac and cheese equally among four microwave safe portable containers. To reheat simply microwave for 1 minute, stir, microwave for an additional 30 seconds to 1 minute, and enjoy!

Nutrition Facts (Per serving)

Calories: 248
Fat: 9g
Carbs: 25g
Protein: 19g
Sodium: 600mg
Sugar: 9g

Mediterranean and Broccoli Pasta

LOW FAT
2 Servings |Prep-time: 10 minutes |Cook-time: 15 minutes

Ingredients

2 cups dry bow tie pasta

1/2 tablespoon olive oil

1/2 cup red onion, diced

2 cups broccoli florets

1 cup sliced white mushrooms

2 cloves garlic, minced

2 Roma tomatoes, chopped into bit-sized pieces

1/2 cup roasted red pepper

1/4 teaspoon each, salt and pepper

1/2 teaspoon crushed red pepper flakes

1 teaspoon garlic powder

1/4 cup low-fat feta or parmesan cheese

Instructions:

1) Cook pasta according to package directions.

2) Meanwhile, heat olive oil in a nonstick pan over medium heat. Once hot, add onion, broccoli, mushrooms, and garlic. Cook until broccoli is tender, about ten minutes.

3) Once broccoli is cooked, add tomatoes, roasted red pepper, salt, pepper, red pepper flakes, and garlic powder. Stir to combine. Transfer to a large mixing bowl.

4) Add cooked pasta to the mixing bowl and veggies and mix to make sure there is an even distribution of all ingredients. Stir in cheese last.

5) You can enjoy this meal right away, or divide into two separate, microwave safe, portable containers.

6) To reheat, simply microwave for 1 minute, stir and microwave for an additional 30 seconds, enjoy!

Nutrition Facts (Per serving)

Calories: 394
Fat: 7.5g
Carbs: 68g
Protein: 16.5g
Sodium: 950mg
Sugar: 11.5g

Eggplant Rollatini

2 Servings |Prep-time: 15 minutes |Cook-time: 25 minutes

Ingredients:

2 large eggplants
1 cup low-fat ricotta cheese
2 tablespoons fat-free milk
1/4 cup low-fat shredded mozzarella cheese
1 tablespoon fresh or dried parsley
1/2 teaspoon garlic powder
1/4 teaspoon each, salt and pepper
1 cup pasta sauce

Instructions:

1) Preheat oven to 375 degrees. Slice eggplants lengthwise so that you have long, wide sheets, about 1/4 inch thick. (You may have to discard the outer pieces as they may not be wide enough. You want about four pieces of eggplant per serving.) Once eggplant is cut, set aside.

2) Add ricotta cheese to a mixing bowl and add milk, mozzarella cheese, parsley, garlic powder, and salt and pepper. Mix until everything is well combined.

3) Lay eggplant pieces down and spread the ricotta mixture over each piece of eggplant. Roll eggplants and place a toothpick through the middle to ensure they stay rolled while cooking.

4) Take a nonstick baking dish and pour pasta sauce onto the bottom, lay eggplants into the dish and transfer to the oven. Bake for 25 minutes, until the eggplant is tender but still firm.

5) Enjoy eggplant right away or divide evenly into two microwaveable portable containers. To reheat, simply microwave for 1 1/2 minutes or until eggplants are warm through the center, enjoy.

Nutrition facts (per serving):

Calories: 247
Fat: 14g
Carbs: 35g
Protein: 20g
Sodium: 1541mg
Sugar: 19g

Four Bean Salad over Arugula

> **LOW FAT**
> **2 Servings | Prep-time: 10 minutes | Cook-time: n/a**

Ingredients:

1 cup canned green beans
1/2 cup canned red kidney beans
1/2 cup canned white beans
1/2 cup canned chickpeas
2 ribs celery
1/2 cup red pepper
1/4 small red onion
1/2 cup low-fat Italian dressing
6 cups arugula

Instructions:

1) Place green beans, kidney beans, white beans, and chickpeas in a strainer and rinse to get rid of any additional sodium. Transfer the beans to a large mixing bowl.

2) Slice celery ribs into thin slices, chop onion into fine dices. Add to the mixing bowl, along with the dressing and stir to combine well.

3) Place three cups of arugula on each plate and top with half of the bean mixture. You can enjoy right away or place the salad in portable containers and refrigerate until you are ready to enjoy.

Nutrition Fats (Per serving):

Calories: 300
Fat: 6g
Carbs: 49g
Protein: 14g
Sodium: 1080mg
Sugar: 15g

Vegetable Fried Rice

> **LOW FAT**
> **2 Servings |Prep-time: 12 minutes |Cook-time: 12 minutes**

Ingredients:

2 ribs celery

1 small onion

2 large carrots

2 teaspoons vegetable oil

1 cup sliced white mushrooms

2 cloves garlic

2 cups pre-cooked brown rice

4 egg whites

1/2 teaspoon dried ground ginger

¼ cup chicken broth

1 teaspoon garlic powder

2 tablespoons soy sauce

Instructions:

1) Preheat a pan or wok over medium-high heat. Slice celery, onion, and carrots into thin pieces. Place oil in pan and add celery, onion, carrots, mushrooms, and garlic. Cook, stirring often, until the vegetables have softened, about ten minutes.

2) Add the brown rice and chicken broth and stir. Once the rice is hot, add the egg white and stir well. Cook for two minutes, until the egg whites are fully cooked. Stir in the ginger, garlic, and soy sauce and remove from heat. Enjoy right away or separate evenly into two microwave safe portable containers. To reheat, simply microwave for 1 - 1 1/2 minutes and enjoy.

Nutrition Facts (Per serving);

Calories: 364
Fat: 7g
Carbs: 60g
Protein: 16g
Sodium: 1526mg
Sugar: 7g

Fiesta Mason Jar Salad

LOW FAT
1 Servings | Prep-time: 5-10 minutes | Cook-time: n/a

Ingredients:

1 large mason jar
3 tablespoons low-fat dressing of choice
1/4 cup canned black beans
1/4 cup canned or frozen corn
4 cups romaine lettuce
2 tablespoons cilantro
1 green onion
1 pre-grilled skinless, boneless, chicken breast
2 tablespoons shredded low-fat cheddar cheese

Instructions:

1) Add dressing to the bottom of the Mason jar. Rinse the black beans and corn to remove any excess sodium and place inside the Mason jar, on top of the

dressing. You want to make sure to layer in this way so that the dressing does not make the lettuce soggy before you enjoy it.

2) Place lettuce on top of the beans and corn. Chop cilantro and green onion and place on top of the lettuce. Chop the chicken breast into small, bite-sized pieces and place in the Mason jar along with the shredded cheddar cheese.

3) Place the cover on the Mason jar and refrigerate until you are ready to enjoy. When you are ready to eat, simply shake the jar to distribute all of the ingredients and coat everything with the dressing, enjoy!

Nutrition Facts:

Calories: 374
Fat: 10g
Carbs: 33g
Protein: 41g
Sodium: 898mg
Sugar: 13

Vegetarian Southwest Salad

1 Servings |Prep-time: 12 minutes |Cook-time: n/a

Ingredients:

4 cups shredded romaine lettuce
1 Roma tomato
1/4 medium avocado
1/4 cup fresh cilantro
1/2 cup canned black beans
1/4 cup low-fat shredded cheddar cheese
2 tablespoons diced red onion
1/4 cup salsa
2 tablespoons low-fat sour cream

Instructions:

1) Lay the lettuce down onto your serving dish or in a portable container if you are making this for on-the-go. Chop Roma tomato and avocado into small diced. Wash the cilantro, pat dry with a paper towel and

chop roughly. Drain 1/2 cup canned black beans into a strainer and rinse to remove excess sodium.

2) Top the lettuce with all ingredients and enjoy!

Nutrition

Calories: 378
Fat: 16g
Carbs: 33
Protein: 24g
Sodium: 894mg
Sugar: 12

French Onion Soup

LOW FAT

2 Servings | Prep-time: 5 minutes | Cook-time: 30 minutes

Ingredients:

2 teaspoons olive oil

2 large Vidalia onions

2 cups reduced-sodium beef broth

1/4 teaspoon pepper

1/2 teaspoon ground thyme

2 slices light pumpernickel bread

2 slices, thin-sliced low-fat Swiss cheese

Instructions:

1) Peel the onions and slice in half. Slice each half into very thin slices. Heat the olive oil in a saucepan over medium heat and add the onions. Cook the onions, stirring often, until soft, about 15 minutes.

2) Once onions are soft, add broth, pepper, and thyme. Reduce heat to low and cook for an additional 15 minutes.

3) Once soup is hot, separate evenly into two oven safe bowls or crocks. Top with a slice of bread and a slice of cheese. Broil for two minutes, until cheese is melted and golden brown.

(You can also enjoy this without broiling by simply placing the bread on a baking sheet, topping each slice of bread with a slice of cheese, and baking for 5 minutes at 375, or until the cheese is melted and golden. Then simply add this on top of your bowl of soup and enjoy!)

Nutrition Facts (Per serving)

Calories: 200
Fat: 8g
Carbs: 25g
Protein: 8g
Sodium: 922mg
Sugar: 5g

Crock Pot Lentil Soup

LOW FAT

3 Servings | Prep-time: 15 minutes | Cook-time: 6-8 hours

Ingredients:

1 Vidalia onion

3 large carrots

3 stalks celery

2 cloves garlic, minced

1 cup dry lentils

1 14.5 ounce can diced tomatoes

6 cups water

1 tablespoon ground cumin

2 bay leafs

2 teaspoons dried ground thyme

1/2 teaspoon each, salt and pepper

1 teaspoon garlic powder

1/2 teaspoon crushed red pepper flakes

1/2 cup grated parmesan cheese

Instructions:

1) Peel the onion, slice in half to make it easier to cut, and then dice each half into very fine dices. Peel the carrot using a vegetable peeler, rinse the celery stalks in water and slice them all into small pieces.

2) Place onion, carrot and celery into the crockpot. Add all of the remaining ingredients, except the parmesan cheese, into the crockpot as well and stir using a wooden spoon or rubber spatula to make sure all ingredients are well combined.

3) Turn crockpot to high heat and allow to cook for about 6-8 hours. This is a perfect recipe to throw everything into the crockpot in the morning and the soup will be ready when you get home from work.

4) Enjoy soup right away topped with a 2 tablespoons of grated parmesan cheese per serving, or scoop servings into microwave safe portable plastic or glass containers, and top with cheese.

5) To reheat, simply place your pre-portioned container of soup in the microwaves for 1 minutes, stir and microwave for an additional minute. Enjoy!

*This recipe makes about 2 cups per serving.

Nutrition facts (Per serving)

Calories: 241
Fat: 3.5g
Carbs: 39g
Protein: 17.5g
Sodium: 1,000mg
Sugar: 6g

Thank you for your interest in my book. I have spent years trying to find the perfect meals to cook that will taste good, satisfy my boys, keep my husband happy (he is an avid cyclist and a health nut) and help me to stay on track with my own dieting goals. The recipes in this book are all easy to prepare, they use healthy ingredients and you can freeze or refrigerate them for later consumption. I try to plan out my week each Sunday but that never seems to work out. These recipes give me a change to get ahead of myself and have a few extra meals standing by for lunch or dinner when needed.

If you enjoyed these recipes, you should check out my other book the Carb Cycling Recipe and Diet Book, you can find it on Amazon. It includes more great recipes, loads of nutrition information, a complete guide to the Carb Cycling Diet and a 26 week diet journal.

Please reach out to me if you have any questions, comments or suggestions and finally if you have a chance please take a moment to post a review on amazon.com, 4 and 5 star reviews really do help promote the book to other readers.

Jesse Morgan
www.FitRecipe.Net

Made in the USA
Lexington, KY
30 December 2014